R. L. Stine

Neil Purslow

www.av2books.com

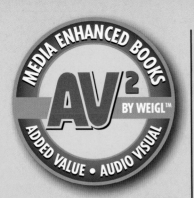

MEDIA ENHANCED BOOKS
AV2 BY WEIGL™
ADDED VALUE • AUDIO VISUAL

AV² provides enriched content that supplements and complements this book. Weigl's AV² books strive to create inspired learning and engage young minds in a total learning experience.

Your AV² Media Enhanced books come alive with...

Audio
Listen to sections of the book read aloud.

Key Words
Study vocabulary, and complete a matching word activity.

Go to www.av2books.com, and enter this book's unique code.

Video
Watch informative video clips.

Quizzes
Test your knowledge.

BOOK CODE

W639081

Embedded Weblinks
Gain additional information for research.

Slide Show
View images and captions, and prepare a presentation.

AV² by Weigl brings you media enhanced books that support active learning.

Try This!
Complete activities and hands-on experiments.

... and much, much more!

Published by AV² by Weigl
350 5th Avenue, 59th Floor
New York, NY 10118
Website: www.weigl.com www.av2books.com

Library of Congress Cataloging-in-Publication Data
Purslow, Neil.
 R. L. Stine / Neil Purslow.
   pages cm. -- (Remarkable Writers)
 Includes index.
 Summary: "Part of a biography series that profiles children's authors of the twentieth century. Explores the life of R. L. Stine and his most popular books, with additional facts provided through a timeline, awards, and fan information. Includes photographs, creative writing tips, and instruction on how to write a biography report. Intended for fourth to sixth grade students"--Provided by publisher.
 ISBN 978-1-62127-404-9 (hardcover : alk. paper) -- ISBN 978-1-62127-410-0 (softcover : alk. paper)
 1. Stine, R. L.--Juvenile literature. 2. Authors, American--20th century--Biography--Juvenile literature. 3. Children's stories--Authorship--Juvenile literature. I. Title.
 PS3569.T4837Z89 2013
 813'.54--dc23
 [B]
                          2012041275

Printed in the United States of America, in North Mankato, Minnesota
1 2 3 4 5 6 7 8 9 0 17 16 15 14 13

012013
WEP301112

Senior Editor: Heather Kissock
Design: Terry Paulhus

Weigl acknowledges Getty Images as its primary photo supplier for this title.

Contents

Introducing
R. L. Stine

When Robert Lawrence Stine was seven years old, he crept into the attic of his house. He worried that he might meet an attic monster. Luckily, there was no monster. He had hoped to find some mysterious trunks, eerie moose heads, or flying bats. Instead, he found his parents' old clothes. However, there was one small black case on the floor. He wondered what was inside.

Robert (Bob) opened the case and made an amazing discovery. Inside was a portable typewriter. Soon, his mother appeared. She had told Bob the attic was not safe. As punishment, Bob was sent to his room. However, his mother let him take the typewriter. He quickly began typing—with one finger.

R. L. Stine likes to meet the people who read his books. He often attends book fairs to meet his fans.

Writing A Biography

Writers are often inspired to record the stories of people who lead interesting lives. The story of another person's life is called a biography. A biography can tell the story of any person, from authors such as R. L. Stine, to inventors, presidents, and sports stars.

When writing a biography, authors must first collect information about their subject. This information may come from a book about the person's life, a news article about one of his or her accomplishments, or a review of his or her work. Libraries and the internet will have much of this information. Most biographers will also interview their subjects. Personal accounts provide a great deal of information and a unique point of view. When some basic details about the person's life have been collected, it is time to begin writing a biography.

As you read about R. L. Stine, you will be introduced to the important parts of a biography. Use these tips and the examples provided to learn how to write about an author or any other remarkable person.

Bob visits bookstores to promote his work. Before he arrives, the stores set up big displays to showcase his books.

Today, Bob is one of the best-selling children's authors in the world. He has sold more than 250 million books in the Goosebumps **series** and more than 80 million books in the Fear Street series. Bob continues to develop new book and series ideas. He has even written books for adults. As busy as he is, he still types with one finger.

Early Life

Robert Lawrence Stine was born in Columbus, Ohio, on October 8, 1943. He grew up in Bexley, Ohio. Bob lived in a three-story house near railroad tracks. His parents worked hard. Bob's father, Lewis, worked for a restaurant supply company. His mother, Anne, stayed home to look after Bob, his younger brother, Bill, and his sister, Pam.

"Time to go to sleep," Bob would say to his brother, Bill, right in the middle of telling a scary story. Bill always wanted to know what happened next. However, Bob would pretend to go to sleep. He liked leaving his brother in suspense.

From an early age, Bob loved comic books. His mother would not let him have comic books because she thought they were not well written. Then, Bob realized that he could read *Mad* and all his other favorite magazines at the barber shop. Almost every Saturday morning, Bob would ask his mother for money to get a haircut. After he had finished reading the new magazines, he would get his hair cut and head home.

Columbus lies along the shores of the Scioto and Olentangy Rivers. It was named the capital of Ohio in 1816.

At home, Bob spent most of his time creating his own comic books and magazines. His first magazine was called *The All New Bob Stine Giggle Book*. It was 10 pages long with five pages of jokes and riddles. Bob typed the words using the old typewriter from the attic. He made many magazines using pens, pencils, crayons, tape, paste, scissors, a stapler, and the typewriter. Bob only made one copy of each magazine. They were a great deal of work. He would give the magazines to his friends to read.

Bob and Bill shared a bedroom when they were children. They would lie in bed and look at the shadows on the walls and ceiling. Then they took turns telling stories about ghosts, haunted houses, bats, werewolves, and mummies. The brothers tried to frighten each other.

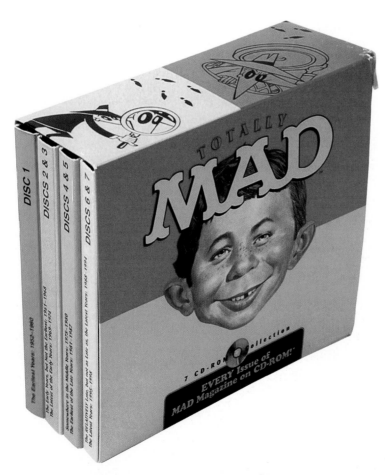

Mad began as a comic book before it became a magazine. Today, people can buy the entire magazine collection as a CD box set.

Growing Up

From an early age, Bob liked scary things. One of his earliest memories is that of a voice from the popular radio show *Suspense*. Each episode of *Suspense* told a different scary story. He would listen to the show until he became too frightened. Then he would turn off the radio. He would wait a few minutes to build up his courage. Then he would turn on the radio again.

Bob also liked to read **science fiction**. He especially enjoyed stories written by Isaac Asimov, Ray Bradbury, and Robert Sheckley. As Bob grew older, he read everything from fairy tales to myths and legends. He had very little interest in reading about real people and places.

Get to Know Central Ohio

Lake Michigan

MICHIGAN

Lake Erie

PENNSYLVANIA

OHIO

INDIANA

Columbus ⭐ •Bexley

ILLINOIS

WEST VIRGINIA

VIRGINIA

KENTUCKY

N W E S

MAP LEGEND

☐ Central Ohio
⊓ State Borders
▨ Land
⭐ Capital City
☐ Water
• Town

0   62.1 MILES
0   100   KILOMETERS

Every Sunday, Bob and Bill would head down to the local theater to see a **horror** movie. They enjoyed the 1950s thrillers *It Came from Beneath the Sea*, *Night of the Living Dead*, and *The Creature from the Black Lagoon*. His favorite movies featured monsters destroying major cities.

When Bob was 13 years old, he began to prepare for his **bar mitzvah**. His parents wanted to buy him a special gift. Bob asked for a new typewriter. They bought him a good quality typewriter that he used for many years.

The monster from *The Creature from the Black Lagoon* gave Bob thrills and chills.

Writing About Growing Up

Some people know what they want to achieve in life from a very young age. Others do not decide until much later. In any case, it is important for biographers to discuss when and how their subjects make these decisions. Using the information they collect, biographers try to answer the following questions about their subjects' paths in life.

1 Who had the most influence on the person?

2 Did he or she receive assistance from others?

3 Did the person have a positive attitude?

Developing Skills

As a teenager, Bob continued to create and publish his own magazines, such as *HAH, for Maniacs Only!* It **spoofed** many popular television shows. In one case, a popular show called *The $64,000 Question* became *The $64,000 Answer*. In another, *Dragnet* became *Dragnut*. This was followed by *Tales to Drive You Batty* and *Whammy*. Next came *Bozos on Patrol, Stine's Line*, and *BARF*. In these last three creations, Bob attached funny **captions** to pictures he cut out of magazines.

"My job is to make kids laugh and give them the creeps!"
—R. L. Stine

Jack Webb and Harry Morgan starred in television's *Dragnet*. Bob would later spoof the show in his own writings.

During his junior and senior high school years, Bob continued to watch scary movies and read frightening books. However, he wanted to make a career out of writing funny stories. Bob was accepted to Ohio State University in 1961. He became the **editor** of the university's **humor** magazine, *Sundial*, in his second year at the college.

Sundial made fun of living at college. Bob became known as Jovial Bob because of his humor and **practical jokes**. The magazine did very well under Jovial Bob's leadership. It became the number one college magazine in the United States in 1965.

Ohio State University was founded in 1870. It is one of the largest universities in the United States.

Writing About Developing Skills

Every remarkable person has skills and traits that make him or her noteworthy. Some people have natural talent, while others practice diligently. For most, it is a combination of the two. One of the most important things that a biographer can do is to tell the story of how the subject developed his or her talents.

1. What was the person's education?

2. What was the person's first job or work experience?

3. What obstacles did the person overcome?

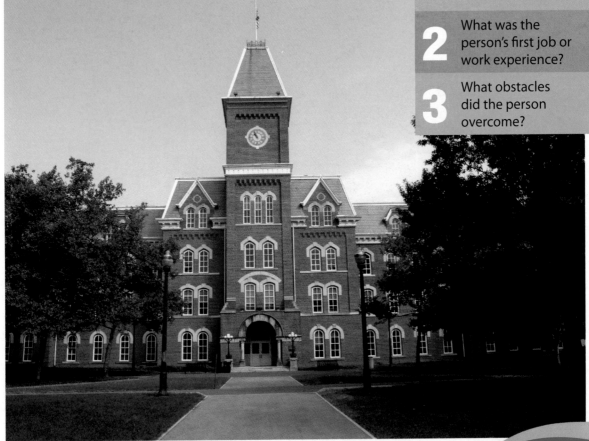

Timeline of R. L. Stine

1969
Bob marries Jane Waldhorn.

1968
Scholastic hires Bob as a staff writer.

1943
Robert Lawrence Stine is born on October 8, in Columbus, Ohio.

1961
Bob enters Ohio State University and becomes "Jovial Bob."

1966
Bob moves to New York City and begins writing for magazines.

1965
Bob graduates from college and becomes a teacher.

1989

With the publication of *The New Girl*, Bob's Fear Street series is launched.

1975

Bananas, a humor magazine that Bob creates and edits, is launched.

1992

Welcome to Dead House, the first book in the Goosebumps series, is released.

1986

His first horror novel, *Blind Date*, is published.

2000

A new series called Nightmare Room is launched.

1978

Bob writes his first children's book, *How to Be Funny*.

1980

Matthew, Bob and Jane's only child, is born.

1984

Bob becomes a **freelance writer.**

Early Achievements

When Bob graduated from college, he became a substitute teacher. He wrote that being a substitute teacher was "scarier than the scariest walk down Fear Street!" While teaching, Bob wrote a two-minute comedy for radio. It was called *Captain Anything*. He had two popular radio hosts from Columbus, Ohio, provide the voices. Then he sent a recording sample to radio stations across the United States. No one would air his show.

By 1966, Bob had saved enough money to move to New York City. One of his first jobs was working for the editor of six teenage fan magazines. Bob wrote a number of interviews with big stars of the 1960s, including the Beatles, Tom Jones, the Rolling Stones, and the Jacksons. However, he never met any of these stars. All of the interviews were imaginary. At the same time, Bob wrote his first horror stories. He authored "Bony Fingers from the Grave," "Trapped in the Vampire's Web of Icy Death," and "It Takes Two for Terror" for a new magazine. However, the magazine was shut down before his stories could be published.

Bob loved listening to scary programs on the radio when he was a child.

After working for a magazine called *Soft Drink Industry,* Bob became a **staff writer** for Junior Scholastic magazines. During his time at Scholastic, Bob met Jane Waldhorn. They married in 1969 and have one son, Matthew.

In 1975, Bob was asked to start a humor magazine for teenagers. It was called *Bananas. Bananas* offered such articles as "How to Turn Your Uncle into a Coffee Table," "How to Tell If You Are an Alien from Outer Space," and "How to Turn Your Poems into Dog Food." Bob was living his dream of writing humor.

Scholastic is one of the world's largest children's publishers. The company was formed in 1920 by Maurice R. "Robbie" Robinson.

Writing About Early Achievements

No two people take the same path to success. Some people work very hard for a long time before achieving their goals. Others may take advantage of a fortunate turn of events. Biographers must make special note of the traits and qualities that allow their subjects to succeed.

1 What was the person's most important early success?

2 What processes does the person use in his or her work?

3 Which of the person's traits were most helpful in his or her work?

Tricks of the Trade

The process for writing **fiction** is different for each author. There is no best way—only what works well for the writer. Each writer has to find his or her own style. Here are some things to think about as you write.

Use Your Past Experiences for Ideas

Use things that you remember from the past to help you create ideas for your stories. Things that scared Bob in the past often became ideas he used in his stories. For instance, many children believe a monster lives in the basement. Bob had the same fear. He used this experience to help him write the Goosebumps story *I Live in Your Basement*.

Stretch Your Imagination

Once you have an idea, fire up your imagination. You can expand that simple idea to create a story plot or chapter. Try putting ordinary characters into situations that they would not normally experience. Your story's main character might become involved in a great deal of trouble. Add more characters to the mix. Have other characters dream up ways to help your main character solve his or her problem.

📝 Like Bob, children can use their imagination to write exciting stories.

Organize Your Thoughts and Ideas

Once you have a plot and some ideas, they need to be organized. Bob uses an **outline** for his stories. His outline contains everything that happens in the book. It even includes the chapter endings. Once the outline is complete, he begins writing. The outline ensures that the story ideas are in the right order. It also ensures that all ideas are included in the story. Bob did not prepare outlines when he first started writing books. He now prepares one for every book he writes.

"I think everyone has imagination, but at the same time, it's a very mysterious process. When I was nine, I was drawn to scary programs and would listen to science fiction shows on the radio. I really can't explain why I found that stuff so interesting. I think I absorbed all those and the many Ray Bradbury stories I read growing up."
—R. L. Stine

Practice, Practice, Practice

It takes practice to write a good story. Bob began writing books when he was 12 years old. Since those early years, he has been writing constantly. When he began writing horror stories, Bob read books by other horror authors to learn how they wrote. His first horror book took him nearly five months to complete. Through practice, Bob is now able to complete an outline and write a book in the Fear Street and Goosebumps series in about 10 or 11 days.

Reading stories written by others can help aspiring authors become better writers.

Remarkable Books

Bob has written many stories. He has authored more than 80 books in the Goosebumps series. The following are some of his favorite books.

Night of the Living Dummy

In *Night of the Living Dummy*, Lindy finds a ventriloquist's dummy and names it Slappy. Slappy is quite ugly, but he is still a lot of fun. Lindy is having a great time learning to make Slappy move and talk. However, Lindy's sister, Kris, is jealous of the attention Lindy and her dummy are getting. Kris decides to get her own dummy. Soon, weird things begin to happen.

AWARDS
Goosebumps series
2000 Second on National Education Association list of kids' favorite books

Don't Forget Me

Danielle, her parents, and younger brother, Peter, have just moved into a new home. Danielle finds her brother annoying and sometimes wishes she was an only child. One night, when her parents are not at home, Danielle hears voices calling from the basement. Her dream to be an only child becomes a nightmare.

The Haunted Mask

In *The Haunted Mask*, Steve Boswell wants to have the scariest costume on the block. He buys a mask that looks like a creepy old man with stringy hair, a wrinkled face, and spiders crawling out of his ears. But Steve finds it may be more than a mask. He begins feeling old, tired, and evil.

Stay Out of the Basement

Dr. Brewer is testing plants in his basement. He says his work is harmless. However, his children are worried. Margaret and Casey Brewer become concerned when they see some of the plants. They also begin to notice that their father is becoming more like his plants. It is up to Margaret and Casey to discover whether their father's work really is safe.

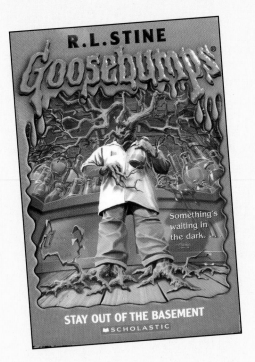

Hide and Shriek

Do you believe in ghosts? Randy Clay has just moved to Fear Street in a strange town called Shadyside. Every year, the town celebrates the birthday of a boy named Pete, who died years ago. The children in town play a game of "hide and shriek" with Pete's ghost in the woods at night. When Pete tags someone, he lives in their body for the next year. As the game begins this year, Randy hears footsteps behind her and feels breathing on her neck. She runs to the cemetery to avoid being tagged. Is she fast enough?

Switched

In *Switched*, Nicole always thought her friend Lucy's life was so much better than her own. She had cooler parents and a cuter boyfriend. Next to Lucy, Nicole felt badly about herself. So when Lucy asked if she wanted to switch bodies, Nicole thought it sounded like a fun idea. At least it would be good for a laugh. What she did not realize is that the plan to trade bodies would actually work—or that Lucy's life might not be so terrific after all. It turns out that Lucy has some problems, and she is about to take revenge—using Nicole's body.

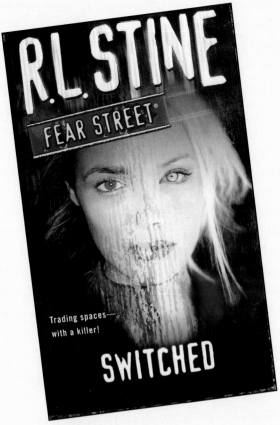

The Face

Martha was in a horrible accident, and she cannot remember what happened to her. Her friends will not talk about it. They say she will remember in time. However, someone wants her to remember immediately. Martha draws this person's face over and over. It is the face of a dead boy she does not know. Martha finds she cannot control her hand as she draws the boy's face, and she cannot remember how he died. She is determined to find the answer.

From Big Ideas to Books

One day, Bob's phone rang. It was an editor from E.P. Dutton, a publisher of children's books. The editor enjoyed reading *Bananas* and thought it was funny. She wanted Bob to write a funny children's book. After many weeks of thinking about ideas, he decided on the title *How to Be Funny*. It would be a very silly guidebook to help children be funny. The book was published in 1978. This was Bob's first book.

"Someone once called me the 'Jekyll and Hyde of children's books.' I guess that's about right. I wrote about 30 or 40 joke books and humor books before I slipped into my 'horror' identity. These days, I'm scary all the time."

—Bob Stine

In 1984, *Bananas* went out of business. Bob then became a full-time freelance writer. He wrote joke books, including *101 Silly Monster Jokes, Sick of Being Sick,* and *Bored of Being Bored*. He also wrote GI Joe action stories, Indiana Jones novels, junior James Bond books, and mystery books. *Madballs* was a series of books Bob wrote about rubber balls with faces. "Somebody's got to write that stuff," he has said of his books.

The Publishing Process

Publishing companies receive hundreds of **manuscripts** from authors each year. Only a few manuscripts become books. Publishers must be sure that a manuscript will sell many copies. As a result, publishers reject most of the manuscripts they receive. Once a manuscript has been accepted, it goes through

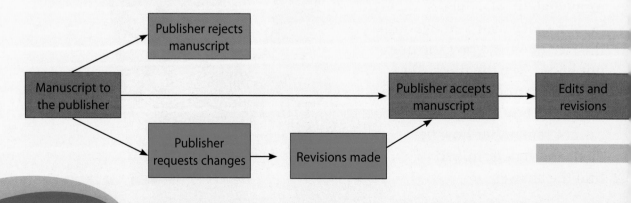

nickelodeon™

Bob was then asked to become the lead writer of a preschool children's television program. It was called *Eureeka's Castle*. After his first year, the show won an Ace Award for best children's show on cable television.

In 1986, Bob had lunch with a publisher. She asked Bob if he had ever thought about writing horror novels for teenagers. Bob had always liked horror but had never thought of writing these types of books. He began by researching similar novels.

However, Bob wanted his book to be funnier and less **gory** than others. He also wanted to write for an 8- to 12-year-old audience. After about five months, the horror novel *Blind Date* was finished. It was published in 1986. Bob decided to use the name R. L. Stine for his horror books since it was scarier than Jovial Bob.

many stages before it is published. Often, authors change their work to follow an editor's suggestions. Once the book is published, some authors receive royalties. This is money based on book sales.

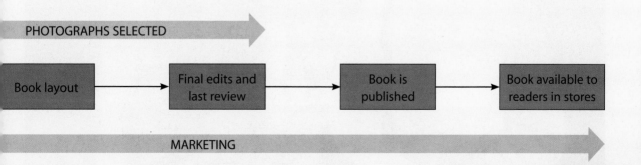

PHOTOGRAPHS SELECTED

| Book layout | → | Final edits and last review | → | Book is published | → | Book available to readers in stores |

MARKETING

R. L. Stine Today

*B*lind Date was a **bestseller.** The publisher asked Bob to write another horror book. This one was called *Twisted,* which was soon followed by *The Baby-sitter.* All were bestsellers. Bob had found something that young readers really liked—to be scared.

Bob decided to write a series of books in the horror **genre.** He needed to come up with a name for the series. Fear Street popped into his head. These books would be written for 9- to 14-year-olds. The first book was *The New Girl.* It was published in 1989. This was followed by *The Surprise Party* and *The Overnight.*

Then someone suggested to Bob that he try writing scary books for younger children. Again, he needed to come up with a name for the series. One day, while looking through the television listings, he saw an advertisement for "Goosebumps Week." He decided the name for his new series would be Goosebumps.

The Goosebumps books were developed into a television series. The show ran from 1995 to 1998.

Goosebumps was launched in 1992 with *Welcome to Dead House.* It was an instant success. Millions of copies were sold. The main difference between the two series is that children do not die in the Goosebumps stories. In Fear Street, many teens can perish. Bob spends about 6 days a week working on his scary books.

By the mid-1990s, Bob was writing an average of two books each month. Even with this workload, he still had ideas for new series. In 1995, he wrote *Superstitious*, his first book for adults. Other series, such as Mostly Ghostly, Rotten School, and Goosebumps Horrorland were also developed at about this time. In 2012, *Red Rain* was released. This was Bob's second book for adults.

In 2000, Bob launched another series called Nightmare Room. This series also has an interactive website where readers can create their own scary stories.

✍ Readers are given the opportunity to create their own scary stories while visiting the Nightmare Room website.

Writing About Person Today

The biography of any living person is an ongoing story. People have new ideas, start new projects, and deal with challenges. For their work to be meaningful, biographers must include up-to-date information about their subjects. Through research, biographers try to answer the following questions.

1 Has the person received awards or recognition for accomplishments?

2 What is the person's life's work?

3 How have the person's accomplishments served others?

Fan Information

When Bob writes a book, his goal is to scare readers. However, he is sad when he hears that one of his books has given a child a nightmare.

Bob receives thousands of fan letters each week. His favorite fan letter came from a boy who wrote, "Dear R. L. Stine, I've read 40 of your books and I think they're really boring." Despite his boredom, the boy had read 40 of Bob's books. Bob makes sure that everyone who writes to him receives a reply. At one time, he had a staff of five people answering his fan mail.

The R. L. Stine website offers visitors the opportunity to find out more about Bob and his books.

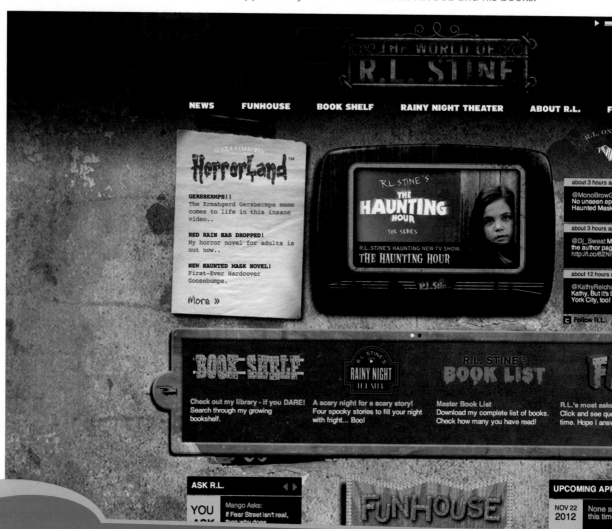

To encourage children to write, Bob has helped set up writing workshops in several of Columbus's public schools. Professional writers come to the schools for 2 weeks each year to work with students who are interested in becoming writers. Bob also visits many children in their classrooms each year. He tells them what it is like to be a writer and encourages them to read and write.

Bob is often invited to major book festivals, where he is asked to talk about his books and the writing process.

Write a Biography

All of the parts of a biography work together to tell the story of a person's life. Find out how these elements combine by writing a biography. Begin by choosing a person whose story fascinates you. You will have to research the person's life by using library books and reliable websites. You can also e-mail the person or write him or her a letter. The person might agree to answer your questions directly.

Use a concept web, such as the one below, to guide you in writing the biography. Answer each of the questions listed using the information you have gathered. Each heading on the concept web will form an important part of the person's story.

Parts of a Biography

Early Life

Where and when was the person born?

What is known about the person's family and friends?

Did the person grow up in unusual circumstances?

Growing Up

Who had the most influence on the person?

Did he or she receive assistance from others?

Did the person have a positive attitude?

Developing Skills

What was the person's education?

What was the person's first job or work experience?

What obstacles did the person overcome?

Person Today

Has the person received awards or recognition for accomplishments?

What is the person's life's work?

How have the person's accomplishments served others?

Early Achievements

What was the person's most important early success?

What processes does the person use in his or her work?

Which of the person's traits were most helpful in his or her work?

Test Yourself

1 When and where was Bob Stine born?

2 When Bob was younger, where did he go every Saturday morning to read comic books and magazines?

3 When Bob went to college, he wrote and edited for an on-campus humor magazine. What was its name?

4 What humor magazine did Bob start when he was with Scholastic?

5 Whom did Bob marry?

6 Bob became the lead writer for which TV show?

7 What is the name of Bob's brother?

8 What was the name of Bob's first horror book?

9 What is the name of the series Bob launched in 2000?

10 What is the name of Bob's most successful series?

Writing Terms

This glossary will introduce you to some of the main terms in the field of writing. Understanding these common writing terms will allow you to discuss your ideas about books and writing with others.

action: the moving events of a work of fiction

antagonist: the person in the story who opposes the main character

autobiography: a history of a person's life written by that person

biography: a written account of another person's life

character: a person in a story, poem, or play

climax: the most exciting moment or turning point in a story

episode: a short piece of action, or scene, in a story

fiction: stories about characters and events that are not real

foreshadow: hinting at something that is going to happen later in the book

imagery: a written description of a thing or idea that brings an image to mind

narrator: the speaker of the story who relates the events

nonfiction: writing that deals with real people and events

novel: published writing of considerable length that portrays characters within a story

plot: the order of events in a work of fiction

protagonist: the leading character of a story; often a likable character

resolution: the end of the story, when the conflict is settled

scene: a single episode in a story

setting: the place and time in which a work of fiction occurs

theme: an idea that runs throughout a work of fiction

Key Words

bar mitzvah: a religious ceremony in which a Jewish boy becomes an adult

bestseller: a book that has extremely high sales

captions: the words that describe pictures in a book, magazine, or newspaper

editor: someone who prepares a manuscript for publication

fiction: characters and events that are not real

freelance writer: a writer who works on his or her own, not as an employee at a company

genre: a specific type or kind of literature

gory: violent or bloody

horror: a feeling of great fear

humor: something that is funny or amusing

manuscripts: drafts of a story before it is published

outline: a summary of everything that happens in a book

practical jokes: tricks played on someone, especially those intended to embarrass the person

science fiction: movies, stories, and books that are fantastic and that make use of scientific devices, space travel, robots, and other things that are real or imagined

series: a set of similar things

spoofed: poked fun at

staff writer: a writer who works as an employee

Index

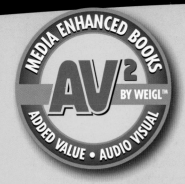

Log on to www.av2books.com

AV² by Weigl brings you media enhanced books that support active learning. Go to www.av2books.com, and enter the special code found on page 2 of this book. You will gain access to enriched and enhanced content that supplements and complements this book. Content includes video, audio, weblinks, quizzes, a slide show, and activities.

AV² Online Navigation

Book Pages
AV² pages directly correspond to pages in the book.

Key Words
Study vocabulary, and complete a matching word activity.

Quizzes
Test your knowledge.

Slide Show
View images and captions, and prepare a presentation.

Audio
Listen to sections of the book read aloud.

Video
Watch informative video clips.

Embedded Weblinks
Gain additional information for research.

Try This!
Complete activities and hands-on experiments.

AV² was built to bridge the gap between print and digital. We encourage you to tell us what you like and what you want to see in the future.

Sign up to be an AV² Ambassador at www.av2books.com/ambassador.